W9-CJG-922

Building
ON A
Dream

THE
Burj
Khalifa

Amie Jane Leavitt

PURPLE TOAD
PUBLISHING

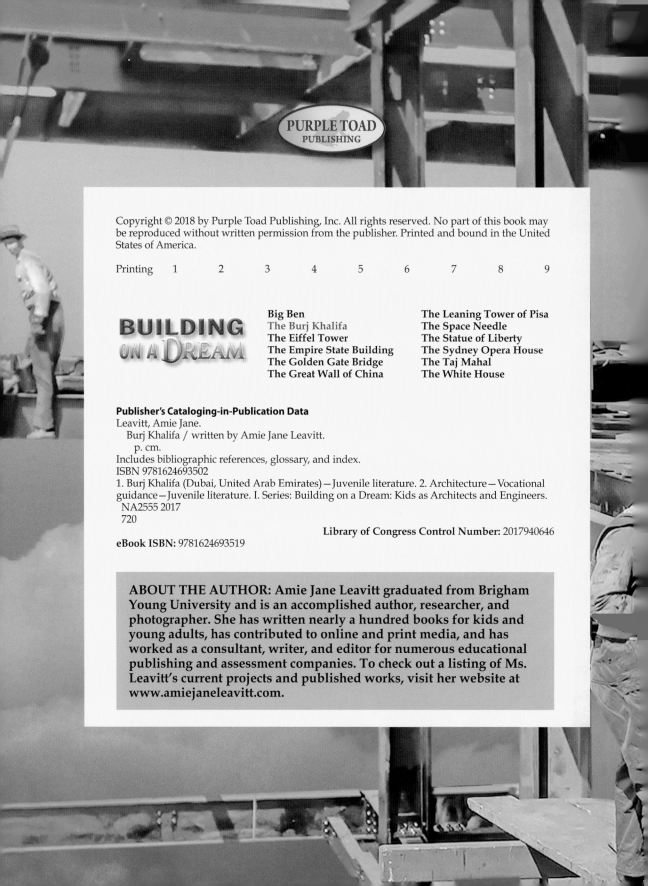

PURPLE TOAD
PUBLISHING

Printing   1   2   3   4   5   6   7   8   9

BUILDING ON A DREAM

Big Ben
The Burj Khalifa
The Eiffel Tower
The Empire State Building
The Golden Gate Bridge
The Great Wall of China

The Leaning Tower of Pisa
The Space Needle
The Statue of Liberty
The Sydney Opera House
The Taj Mahal
The White House

Publisher's Cataloging-in-Publication Data
Leavitt, Amie Jane.
   Burj Khalifa / written by Amie Jane Leavitt.
      p. cm.
Includes bibliographic references, glossary, and index.
ISBN 9781624693502
1. Burj Khalifa (Dubai, United Arab Emirates)—Juvenile literature. 2. Architecture—Vocational guidance—Juvenile literature. I. Series: Building on a Dream: Kids as Architects and Engineers.
 NA2555 2017
 720

Library of Congress Control Number: 2017940646

eBook ISBN: 9781624693519

ABOUT THE AUTHOR: Amie Jane Leavitt graduated from Brigham Young University and is an accomplished author, researcher, and photographer. She has written nearly a hundred books for kids and young adults, has contributed to online and print media, and has worked as a consultant, writer, and editor for numerous educational publishing and assessment companies. To check out a listing of Ms. Leavitt's current projects and published works, visit her website at www.amiejaneleavitt.com.

CONTENTS

The sky over Dubai lit up on January 4, 2010, as the city celebrated the Burj Khalifa's birthday.

A Grand Opening

More than 10,000 fireworks burst in the sky. The multicolored lights splashed and sparkled in front of the 2,722-foot mammoth tower. This day, January 4, 2010, was the grand opening of the Burj Khalifa. The needle-like building soared above the United Arab Emirates city of Dubai.[1]

When the Burj Khalifa was built, it was the tallest building in the world. The next closest building at that time was the Taipei 101 in Taiwan's capital city. It was some 1,055 feet shorter than the Burj Khalifa. To put that into perspective, the Chrysler Building in New York is 1,046 feet tall. If you stacked the Chrysler Building on top of the Taipei 101, then you'd reach the height of the Burj Khalifa.[2]

Until opening day, the general public did not know the exact height of the Burj Khalifa. The builders kept this detail a closely guarded secret. That way, other builders would not try to make an even taller structure before the Burj Khalifa was finished.[3]

Builders did not want another skyscraper war like the one that occurred in New York City during the 1920s and 1930s. That's when the Manhattan Company Building and the Chrysler Building were constructed. These two buildings went up at the same time, and the builders vied to outdo each other on height. Both wanted to build the tallest structure in the world. Ultimately, the Chrysler Building was taller, but its glory lasted only about 11 months. When the Empire State Building was completed in May 1931, it was taller than the Chrysler Building by 200 feet.[4]

The Burj Khalifa is the crowning jewel on the Dubai skyline.

Keeping the height of the Burj Khalifa a secret made opening day that much more exciting. As its windows reflected the sparkling fireworks, huge video screens revealed the ultimate height of the tower. Finally, the number of 828 (meters) was displayed.[5]

Like all other skyscrapers before it, the Burj Khalifa wouldn't be able to hold its world record forever. Other buildings were already in the works that would be taller than the Burj Khalifa. The Jeddah Tower in Saudi Arabia was scheduled to be completed in 2020. It would be almost 600 feet taller than the Burj Khalifa, rising some 3,307 feet into the sky. Other taller buildings were slated to break the Jeddah Tower's record, too. The completion date for Sky Mile Tower in Tokyo was

2045. It would stretch over a mile into the sky, reaching 5,577 feet. That is roughly two Burj Khalifas stacked on top of each other![6]

Constructing a building such as these is a colossal task. About 12,000 people worked on the Burj Khalifa, providing about 22 million man-hours. People came to Dubai from all over the world. Engineers hailed from Europe and the United States. Construction laborers were brought in from India, China, Bangladesh, and Pakistan. Project managers solved language barriers and cultural differences. Team leaders and supervisors were multilingual so that they could communicate with workers and engineers. Since people came to the project from different cultures and religions, the workday sometimes

The Burj Khalifa sits in a 500-acre section of Dubai, beside a mall, hotels, shops and water features.

had to be adjusted. For example, breaks were given during the daytime so that Muslim workers could perform their daily prayers.[7]

An extraordinary amount of material was used to build Burj Khalifa. Thirty-nine thousand tons of steel rebar was used. If placed end to end, these metal bars would stretch a fourth of the way around the earth at its equator. Some 26,000 glass panels were used on the outside of the building. Approximately 431,600 cubic yards of concrete were used in the building's framework. That is enough to pour a sidewalk 55 miles long. The weight of the aluminum used in Burj Khalifa was equal to five A380 aircrafts.[8]

When completed, the Burj Khalifa boasted a total of 5.67 million square feet. It weighs about 500,000 tons, which is the weight of 100,000 elephants! On its 163 floors, some 35,000 people can work or live. There are 900 luxury apartments in the building. A total of 37

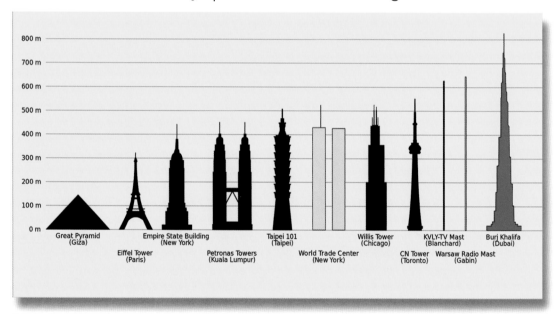

This is how the Burj Khalifa stacks up to earlier man-made structures.

Condensation slides down the building into a tank. Then it is pumped out to water the tower's gardens.

floors are dedicated to office space. There is a glamorous five-star hotel in the building that has a total of 304 rooms. The building also hosts shopping centers, fine-dining restaurants, fitness facilities, indoor and outdoor swimming pools, libraries, and many other features you would find in a town or city.[9]

Besides being the tallest building, the Burj Khalifa has set other world records, too. It is the tallest freestanding structure in the world. It has the most stories of any building in the world. It has the highest occupied floor. It has the highest outdoor observation deck. The Burj Khalifa's highest outside deck is some 1,823 feet above the ground. It also has 57 elevators, one of which travels farther than any other elevator in the world: 1,654 feet.[10]

With innovation, any of those records could be broken when other towers are built. But for a few years, Burj Khalifa would most likely hold on to many of these distinctions.

Sheikh Mohammed bin Rashid Al Maktoum is the ruler of Dubai. He contracted with a company to build the Burj Khalifa.

Dreaming Higher

In 2003, the ruler of Dubai, Sheikh Mohammed bin Rashid Al Maktoum, wanted to create something exciting in his city. He asked a company called Emaar Properties to build a grand tower in an area that would be known as Downtown Dubai. His goal was to make Dubai more attractive to visitors, and he felt that an iconic structure would help. The tower would be mega-tall—the tallest in the world. In his dream, the structure would draw global attention.[1]

To find a designer for the building, Emaar Properties hosted a worldwide competition. The best architectural and engineering firms sent in their ideas. The winning design had been sent in by the firm Skidmore, Owings, and Merrill (SOM), based in the United States. SOM had been in business since 1936. It had designed such impressive structures as the Sears Tower (now Willis Tower) in Chicago and the new One World Trade Center in New York City. The main architect for the winning design was Adrian Smith.

The job of an architect is to come up with what the building will look like. He or she will try to match a building with the place it will be built and for the people who will use it. For example, the Taipei 101 was designed to look like a giant pagoda, which is a traditional tower in China that is used as a temple or memorial. Because the designers chose such a design, the tower fits well with the area. It brings a sense of cultural and geographical identity to a place.[2]

The spider lily's shape inspired the Burj Khalifa's design.

Since the Burj Khalifa would be built in a Muslim nation, Smith decided to use elements of Islamic art in his design. Islamic art blends geometric patterns and shapes from nature. Smith liked the idea of using the *Hymenocallis* flower, or spider lily. He used the shape of this flower as the base of the tower.[3]

The base is the most important part of any building, since it provides stability for the structure. In his design, Smith used a hexagonal (six-sided) center. Extending from there, he included three buttresses or wings. Since these were all attached to the center hexagon, they gave the tower a strong, solid base.

The hexagon and wings formed a Y-shape that looked exactly like the outline of a

Building a solid foundation is the first step in any successful skyscraper project.

spider lily. From above, the tower would look like the onion dome found on Muslim mosques. This unique shape served a useful purpose as well as an artistic one. It would give the best views from inside the building, no matter which window a person was using. The views of the Persian Gulf would be especially stunning.[4]

From this solid and strong base, the tower would rise upward. As it did, each floor was set back ever so slightly so that the completed tower would look like a needle. The tower would also slightly twist as it rose. It would look like a spiraling minaret, another important symbol in the Islamic faith. Minarets are tall, slender towers with one or more balconies that are used to call Muslims to prayer. The gentle twisting shape was an important structural feature of the building, too. It helped prevent even the strongest winds from affecting the building.

At the top of the building, Smith decided to place a spire. This spire would be about 650 feet tall, which is equal to two Statues of Liberty stacked on top of each other. This spire would be hollow and would store various communication and mechanical equipment for the building. It would also give the building the feel of continually climbing toward the heavens as it tapered to a thin point.[5]

The last part of the building's construction was the tall needle-shaped spire.

Bill Baker

Before a building is constructed, a model is built. The model is then put through a variety of tests to see if it can withstand various stresses from wind, earthquakes, and gravity.

Testing the Design

Architects do not work alone in designing buildings. Another important member of the team is the structural engineer. The architect will come up with the initial design, and then the structural engineer will test it and fine-tune it as necessary. The structural engineer uses mathematics, science, and engineering principles to test the design. For the Burj Khalifa, the lead structural engineer was Bill Baker.

When evaluating a design, the structural engineer must take many factors into account. First, gravity can play havoc on a tower. Think about building a tower out of blocks and how quickly it will tumble if it isn't built just right. When structural engineers test design ideas, they figure out whether the tower will stand when the earth pulls on it. They also figure out if the weight of the tower will cause it to sink into the ground. If there are problems with the design, the engineer will suggest ways to fix them.

For the Burj Khalifa, Baker knew the sandy ground would not be stable enough to hold the building. It would either sink or tip over—or both. The engineers decided they would have to make a concrete foundation on which to build the tower. They would pour a special mat of about 13,700 cubic yards of concrete. The mat would rest on 192 concrete piles, which would be driven deep into the earth. Each pile was almost five feet (1.5 m) wide and 140 feet (43 m) tall.[1]

After gravity, engineers have to think about wind—especially on super high towers. The higher a tower gets, the greater the wind will impact it. Wind can make towers sway back and forth. If the building

Wind tunnels are used to see how much wind a building can withstand.

moves too much, the people inside will feel as if they are being tossed around on a ship at sea. If the building moves too little, the wind can crack it or knock it over. Engineers conduct many tests on models to ensure that the building can withstand even the strongest of winds.

For the Burj Khalifa, the engineers performed more than 40 different wind tests. They knew that winds could be very strong in Dubai. Wind at the top of the Burj Khalifa could reach about 150 miles per hour, which is as strong as a major hurricane. The engineers built models of the tower and placed them in wind tunnels to see how they would respond. When anything major happened in the test, the design was changed.[2]

Wind tests were also done on the proposed balconies. The engineers found that the design of these decks would have to be changed so that people would be safe on them. Alarm systems were also installed to let people know if it was too dangerous to go outdoors at any particular time.[3]

Earthquakes are another concern for building designers. Although earthquakes are rare in Dubai, buildings over ten stories high must be built to handle a quake of 5.9 on the Richter scale. Not only does the building have to stay up, but the material that makes up the façade must also stay attached. Again, structural engineers use models to conduct their tests. If the model fails, then the design must be adjusted. After a series of seismic tests on models of the Burj Khalifa, it was found that the tower would be safe up to a 7.0 earthquake.[4]

Another concern for modern buildings is how the sun heats them. Most tall towers are covered in glass panels. These serve as windows and allow natural light into the building. However, the glass also lets in heat from the sun. To keep the heat out, the glass is often covered with certain films. Engineers test these films to ensure they will perform well, and that they will last. These tests were particularly important on the Burj Khalifa, since in Dubai, temperatures can soar far above 100°F. That is enough to turn a glass-covered tower into an oven.[5]

On the observation deck, people can look at video screens to find out what they're looking at on the horizon.

Structural engineers must also plan for emergencies such as fire and power outages. In such a tall tower, how can they make sure that all the people can get out safely? Evacuation plans are thought out, and then the building is designed around them. For example, the Burj Khalifa has a series of staircases connecting the top floor to the ground. They total 2,909 steps.

In the stairwells, fans force clean, fresh air through fireproof air ducts. The fresh air keeps smoke from building up in the stairwells. There are also nine refuge rooms placed throughout the tower. These rooms have fireproof doors that can keep occupants safe for two hours. There is one room about every 25 floors. While it takes a lot of strength to climb up or down 15 flights of stairs, this distance is much easier to travel than the entire height of the building.[6]

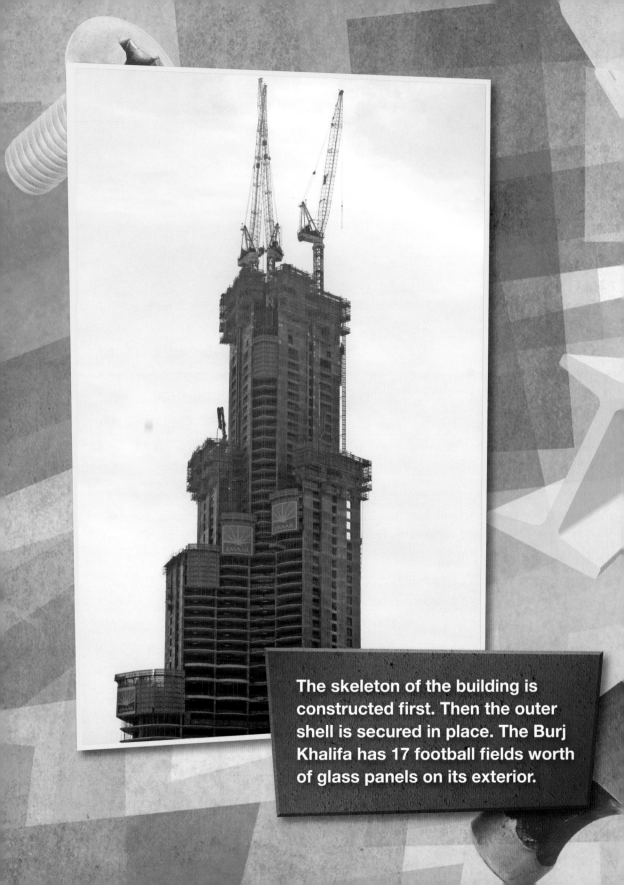

The skeleton of the building is constructed first. Then the outer shell is secured in place. The Burj Khalifa has 17 football fields worth of glass panels on its exterior.

Construction Challenges

A challenge in building tall structures is figuring out how to get people and supplies higher and higher as the tower grows. These issues have been resolved on other building projects, but could these same techniques be used on the Burj Khalifa? This building was completely different from anything that had been built before—the workers and supplies would need to be sent to far greater heights.

One traditional way to get supplies up a tower is by using a crane. Cranes are generally used on construction projects that are taller than one floor. However, special skyscraper cranes had to be used to reach the height of Burj Khalifa. These cranes are called kangaroo cranes. They were invented in Australia, and they can raise themselves up—hopping up three floors at a time—during the building process.[1]

Three kangaroo cranes were used on this job. When the lower floors were being built, the crane rested on the ground and lifted the building supplies to where they were needed. Then, when the tower reached a certain height, the cranes climbed up inside the building as the tower ascended.[2]

Another tricky part in the construction process occurred when the spire was installed. No crane could reach that high. A helicopter was considered, but the spire was far too heavy for a helicopter to lift. In the end, the workers built the spire inside the top of the tower. They then hoisted the spire through the top of the tower using a jack and then set it in place.[3]

The Burj Khalifa was built using concrete and steel. Concrete walls are built using a specific method. First, two metal forms or walls are set up. Steel rebar cages are placed inside the metal forms. Then, concrete is mixed in a big truck, piped through tubes, and poured into the forms. The concrete is left to cure for about 12 hours. Then the forms are removed, and the walls are done. This process works the same way whether the building is one story or one hundred stories.

The challenge in using this method, though, is figuring out how to get the wet concrete up to the highest floors of a skyscraper. Time is of the essence with concrete. If it takes too long to get to the top, it could become solid inside the tubes. The concrete would have to be dumped from the tubes as quickly as possible. Special pumps were

Wet concrete is pumped out of these machines and into the forms to build the walls.

used on the Burj Khalifa that moved the concrete quickly up the tower. In fact, they were the fastest concrete pumps in the world.[4]

Concrete also sets quickly if it gets too hot. The temperatures at the construction site could be as high as 130°F. To buy more time, instead of mixing the concrete with just water, ice was also used. This kept the concrete cool for a longer period of time. Much of the concrete was poured at night, when temperatures were lower.

As the walls were built, a "jump-form" system was used. When the concrete had cured, the forms would be raised to the next level and set into place. Then the walls on that floor could be immediately poured. This speedy construction method allowed workers to build a new floor on Burj Khalifa every three days.[5]

Skyscrapers must be built as quickly as possible. These projects cost a lot of money, and that money cannot be recouped until the building space can be rented. Construction on the Burj Khalifa continued around the clock for a total of 1,325 days—a little more than three and a half years.[6]

Each step of the building process was a marvel to behold.

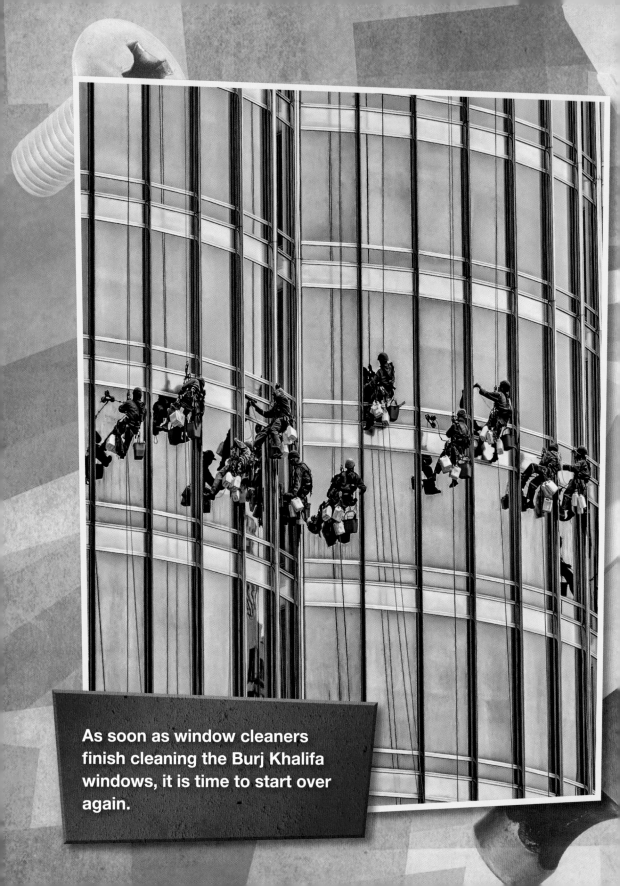

As soon as window cleaners finish cleaning the Burj Khalifa windows, it is time to start over again.

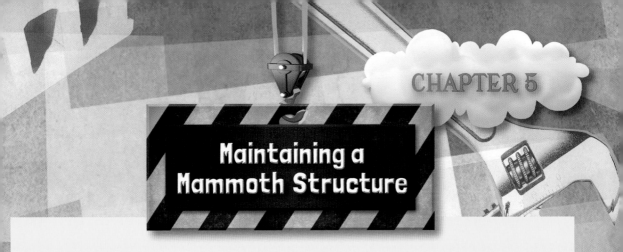

Maintaining a Mammoth Structure

Once a building is constructed, the work is not over. In reality, it has just begun.

Engineers need to constantly monitor the plumbing, electrical, heating, air conditioning, and communication systems in the building. In skyscrapers, effects of the wind, earthquake activity, and gravity forces also have to be watched.

In the Burj Khalifa, teams of engineers constantly monitor the tower. They have offices right inside the building and keep track of everything using computers. When problems arise, they send technicians immediately to the area of the building that needs to be fixed.[1]

Large buildings also need to be cleaned on both the inside and the outside. Teams of cleaning crews work around the clock to clean the 163 floors of living space in the building. In addition, the outside of the building has to be maintained. Dubai is in the middle of the desert, where sandstorms are common. The city is also located next to the Persian Gulf. Without constant cleaning, the Burj Khalifa would be covered in a layer of sand and salt. The shiny exterior would look brown and dull. And the people inside wouldn't be able to see out.

Cleaning the glass panels is done the old-fashioned way: by hand. Workers are hoisted over the top of the tower on ropes. Then they rappel down the sides of the tower, cleaning the windows as they go. It takes a team of 11 people approximately three months to clean the

entire tower. As soon as they are done, they go back to the top and start over again.[2]

Sheikh Mohammed bin Rashid Al Maktoum's dream for his downtown Dubai has come true. People around the world consider the Burj Khalifa to be one of the modern wonders of the world. Almost two million people visit the observation decks every year. They come to the tower to spy amazing views of the city, the Persian Gulf, and the surrounding desert. They walk the grounds at the base of the tower and look up in awe at its impressive architecture. Even if other buildings eventually soar to greater heights, there will never be another building exactly like the Burj Khalifa.[3]

From the top of Burj Khalifa, visitors can spy views of Dubai and the surrounding desert.

The Burj Khalifa soars nearly a half mile into the sky. Its many curved surfaces deflect and weaken strong gusts of wind. They also provide extra windows for wider views.

2003   Sheikh Mohammed bin Rashid Al Maktoum asks Emaar Properties to build a mammoth structure in the new Downtown Dubai area. Emaar Properties conducts a worldwide design competition. The design from Skidmore, Owings, and Merrill is chosen.

2004   January: Excavation is started on the site of the Burj Khalifa.

February: A total of 192 concrete piles are poured, cured, and then drilled into the earth. The concrete pad is poured on top.

2005   March: Construction on the ground floor level is begun.

2006   June: The building is complete up to level 50.

2007   January: Construction up to level 100 has been completed.

March: Burj Khalifa is finished up to floor 110.

April: Construction is now complete up to floor 120.

May: Level 130 of Burj Khalifa is complete.

July: Level 141 has been reached. Burj Khalifa is now officially the tallest building in the world.

September: Construction up to level 150 has been completed. The Burj Khalifa sets another world record. It is the tallest freestanding structure in the world.

2008   April: The Burj Khalifa is now to level 160. It is now the tallest man-made structure in the world.

2009   January: The spire is installed. The Burj Khalifa is now at its total height.

2009   September: All of the glass and aluminum façade has been installed on the building's exterior.

2010   January: Grand opening ceremony of Burj Khalifa, complete with grand fireworks display. The final height of the building is revealed to be 2,722 feet.

Chapter Notes

Chapter 1
1. "National Geographic Mega Structures: Burj Khalifa, Dubai" YouTube video.
2. Ibid.
3. Ibid.
4. "Tale of Two Skyscrapers." Slate.com.
5. "National Geographic Mega Structures: Burj Khalifa, Dubai." YouTube video.
6. "Burj Khalifa." Best Infographics.
7. "How Do You Build the Tallest Building in the World?" Samsung Village.
8. "Building a Global Icon." Burj Khalifa Official Website.
9. "Burj Khalifa." Best Infographics.
10. "Burj Khalifa, the World's Tallest Building, Inaugurated: Global Press and Visitors Ride Otis Elevators to Observation Deck." Otis Worldwide.

Chapter 2
1. "National Geographic Mega Structures: Burj Khalifa, Dubai." YouTube video.
2. Bill Baker. "The Design and Construction of the World's Tallest Building: the Burj Khalifa, Dubai."
3. "National Geographic Mega Structures: Burj Khalifa, Dubai." YouTube video.
4. Baker.
5. "Burj Khalifa." Best Infographics.

Chapter 3
1. Bill Baker. "The Design and Construction of the World's Tallest Building: the Burj Khalifa, Dubai."
2. "National Geographic Mega Structures: Burj Khalifa, Dubai." YouTube video.
3. "Constructing Tallest Building in the World—Burj Khalifa."
4. "Safety Features In The World's Highest Building: The Burj" Code Red Safety.
5. "Constructing Tallest Building in the World – Burj Khalifa." Official HD Documentary 2015. YouTube video.
6. "Safety Features In The World's Highest Building: The Burj."

Chapter 4
1. Marc Santora. "Can We Build a Better Crane?"
2. "Constructing Tallest Building in the World—Burj Khalifa." Official HD Documentary 2015. YouTube video.
3. "National Geographic Mega Structures: Burj Khalifa, Dubai." YouTube video.
4. "Constructing Tallest Building in the World—Burj Khalifa."
5. Ibid.
6. "Burj Khalifa." Best Infographics.

Chapter 5
1. "Burj Khalifa Fact Sheet." At the Top, Burj Khalifa.
2. Bonnie Malkin. "Burj Khalifa: Window Cleaners to Spend Months on World's Tallest Building." Telegaph.co.uk.
3. Rebecca Bundhun. "Burj Khalifa a Towering Tourism Influence." *The National.*

Books

Dupre, Judith. *Skyscrapers: A History of the World's Most Extraordinary Buildings.* New York: Blackdog and Leventhall Publishers, 2013.

Goldsworthy, Kaite. *Burj Khalifa.* New York: Weigl Publishers, 2012.

Graham, Ian. *Megastructures: Tallest, Longest, Biggest, Deepest.* Richmond Hill, Ontario: Firefly Books, 2012.

Kellen, Stuart. *Burj Khalifa: The Tallest Tower in the World.* Chicago: Norwood House Press, 2013.

Smith, A.G. *Burj Khalifa.* Mineola, New York: Dover Publications, 2011.

On the Internet

Burj Khalifa Official Web Site:
http://www.burjkhalifa.ae/

PBS: Building Big, All About Skyscrapers
http://www.pbs.org/wgbh/buildingbig/skyscraper/

Skidmore, Owings & Merrill: Burj Khalifa
http://www.som.com/projects/burj_khalifa

Visit Dubai
http://www.visitdubai.com/

Works Consulted

"40 Wall Street—The Trump Building." *Wired New York.* Retrieved January 26, 2017. http://wirednewyork.com/skyscrapers/40wall/

Baker, Bill. "The Design and Construction of the World's Tallest Building: The Burj Khalifa, Dubai." *Structural Engineering International.* April 2015. https://www.iabse.org/Images/Publications_PDF/SEI/SEI.Burj%20Dubai.pdf

"Building a Global Icon." Burj Khalifa Official Website. Retrieved January 26, 2017. http://www.burjkhalifa.ae/en/the-tower/construction.aspx

Bundhun, Rebecca. "Burj Khalifa a Towering Tourism Influence." *The National.* January 5, 2011. http://www.thenational.ae/business/travel-tourism/burj-khalifa-a-towering-tourism-influence

"Burj Khalifa." *Best Infographics*. February 18, 2012. http://www.bestinfographics. info/burj-khalifa/

"Burj Khalifa Fact Sheet." *At the Top*, Burj Khalifa. Retrieved January 26, 2017. http://www.burjkhalifa.ae/img/FACT-SHEET.pdf

"Burj Khalifa, the World's Tallest Building, Inaugurated: Global Press and Visitors Ride Otis Elevators to Observation Deck." *Otis Worldwide*. Retrieved January 26. 2017. http://www.otis.com/_layouts/ProjectNewsPopup. aspx?ID=13&siteURL=http://www.otis.com/site/in/pages/OtisNews.aspx

"Constructing Tallest Building in the World—Burj Khalifa." Official HD Documentary 2015. YouTube, April 18, 2015. https://www.youtube.com/ watch?v=4mt8SifFqZQ

Hope, Bradley. "High Living at the Burj Khalifa." *The National*. February 22, 2011. http://www.thenational.ae/business/industry-insights/property/high-living-at-the-burj-khalifa

Israel, Brett. "10 Things You Didn't Know About the Burj Khalifa, the New Tallest Building in the World." *Discover Magazine*. January 4, 2010. http://blogs. discovermagazine.com/80beats/2010/01/04/10-things-you-didnt-know-about-the-burj-khalifa-the-new-tallest-building-in-the-world/#.WIoW-BsrKUk

"The Man Behind the Wonders—Bill Baker Reveals the Secrets of Structural Engineering." *Industrial Prime*. June 22, 2016. http://industrialprime.com/ the-man-behind-the-wonders-bill-baker-reveals-the-secrets-of-structural-engineering/

"National Geographic Mega Structures: Burj Khalifa, Dubai" YouTube Video February 6, 2014. https://www.youtube.com/watch?v=yyaEIf2ok6I

Santora, Marc. "Can We Build a Better Crane?" *The New York Times*. June 2, 2008. https://cityroom.blogs.nytimes.com/2008/06/02/can-we-build-a-better-crane/?_r=0

"Tale of Two Skyscrapers." Slate.com. February 6, 2014. http://www.slate.com/ blogs/the_eye/2014/02/06/the_race_to_dominate_the_new_york_city_skyline_higher_by_neal_bascomb.html

buttress (BUH-tress)—An area of stone or brick that provides support.

crane (KRAYN)—Heavy equipment machine with ropes, cables, or chains that is used to lift and move objects.

edifice (EH-di-fis)—A large building or structure.

evacuation (ee-vah-kyoo-AY-shun)—The removal of people from an area of danger.

façade (fah-SAHD)—The outside covering of a building, also known as "fake front." In the Burj Khalifa, the façade is the glass and aluminum curtain on the building that covers up the concrete and steel exoskeleton.

hexagon (HEK-sih-gon)—A six-sided shape. The prefix *hexa* means "six."

hoist (HOYST)—To lift.

iconic (eye-KAH-nik)—Widely recognized; first-rate.

innovation (ih-noh-VAY-shun)—A new method, idea, or product.

Islamic (iz-LAH-mik)—Having to do with the Muslim religion, which follows the teachings of the Prophet Mohammed.

mammoth (MAM-ith)—Super-sized; extremely large.

minaret (MIH-nuh-ret)—One of the tall, slender towers with one or more balconies that are used to call Muslims to prayer.

mosque (MOSK)—Holy places in which Muslims worship.

multilingual (mul-tee-LING-wul)—Able to speak many languages.

pagoda (puh-GOH-duh)—A Hindu or Buddhist temple or sacred building.

pile—Concrete or stone towers that are drilled into the earth and used to support the foundation of a building.

rappel (ruh-PEL)—To descend down a rock, mountain, building, or other vertical surface by using ropes around the body for support.

Richter (RIK-ter) **scale**—A chart to measure the strength of an earthquake.

seismic (SYZ-mik)—Relating to the movement or vibration of the earth, such as are caused by earthquakes.

spire (SPYR)—A tapering cone-shaped, needle-shaped, or pyramid-shaped structure on the top of a building.

PHOTO CREDITS: Cover—Alberto Gonzales Rovira; p. I—John Christian Fjellestad; p. 6—Hisham Binuswaif; p. 7—Milos Milosevic; p. 9—Archie Choong; p. 10—Karim Saad; p. 12—Tatters; p. 13—Imre Solt; p. 17—Marko Kudjerski; p. 18— Ryan Lackey; p. 21—Soonadracula; p. 22—Vikramjit Kakati; p. 24—Daniel Julia Lundgren; p. 25—Portengaround. All other photos—Public Domain. Every measure has been taken to find all copyright holders of material used in this book. In the event any mistakes or omissions have happened within, attempts to correct them will be made in future editions of the book.